£5.25

THANKS
4 THE
Support
PEACE....
Love....
Unity....
TERRY
95

T.H.A.N.K.S
the
Tender Hearts And New Knowledge Suppliers

BRIAN

"When I think of annuals, I think of the Beano annual or those Viz ones. It's a bit strange having an *East 17* one. I mean, are we meant to be some kind of a joke, or what? Seriously though, we did have a laugh with this and we've tried not to make it too deep or anything. It's really meant to be a light-hearted thing, nothing too heavy, and a bit of fun. Plus, if you read my recipes, you could turn out to be as good at cooking as I am. Cheers."

TERRY

"To all of you readers, I hope you like our annual. I hope you'll find some information in it which is different from the normal 'news' you normally read about us everywhere else. It's difficult to always give you stuff that you don't already know, but we've done our best to think of as much as we can. A lot of work has been put into this for you fans out there, and we had a lot of fun getting it all together - so read on!"

JOHN

"I think this annual is a good idea because a lot of the fans don't really get to see a lot of the photographs and they don't really get to know what you're like. A lot of people are really interested to learn what you're personality is like, what you've done in your life so far, or what you're looking forward to doing. Different things like that. I reckon it's great that people can get hold of a book like this so that they can really get to know us for what we are. That's the general idea anyway."

TONY

"The more famous we get, the busier we get and, therefore, the further from our fans, physically, we get. We'd like to keep in touch, and this is the point of having an annual like this. But we don't want to give you the usual stuff you might expect to find in a book like this; we wanted to try and do something completely different. Normally, you look at an annual - and you can guess what's inside it. So we're not going to give you our dates of birth, favourite colours and all of that stuff; you should know that detail by now. We're going to give you something else. Hope you enjoy it..."

CONTENTS

Written by Mike Hrano
Edited by Melanie J Clayden
Design by Susan Bartram
Logo design by Form
Photography by Lawrence Watson

Published by GRANDREAMS LIMITED
Jadwin House, 205-211 Kentish Town Road, London NW5 2JU.

Printed in Italy

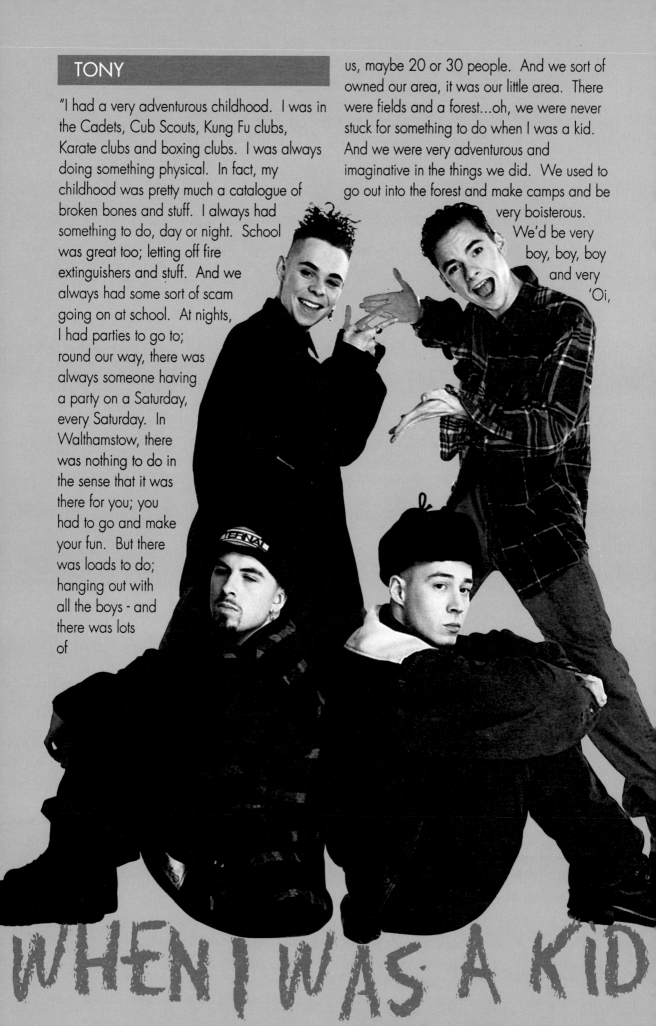

TONY

"I had a very adventurous childhood. I was in the Cadets, Cub Scouts, Kung Fu clubs, Karate clubs and boxing clubs. I was always doing something physical. In fact, my childhood was pretty much a catalogue of broken bones and stuff. I always had something to do, day or night. School was great too; letting off fire extinguishers and stuff. And we always had some sort of scam going on at school. At nights, I had parties to go to; round our way, there was always someone having a party on a Saturday, every Saturday. In Walthamstow, there was nothing to do in the sense that it was there for you; you had to go and make your fun. But there was loads to do; hanging out with all the boys - and there was lots of

us, maybe 20 or 30 people. And we sort of owned our area, it was our little area. There were fields and a forest...oh, we were never stuck for something to do when I was a kid. And we were very adventurous and imaginative in the things we did. We used to go out into the forest and make camps and be very boisterous. We'd be very boy, boy, boy and very 'Oi,

WHEN I WAS A KID

oi! Geezer, geezer!' With our catapults and stuff. And BMX bikes were in fashion then. We'd breakdance too. So, yeah, it was a crazy childhood. A really, really good one. And you learned how to survive, as well. Not in the sad sense, although we certainly didn't have a lot of money, but in terms of facing up to life. Personality-wise, the basis of what I am today was definitely already there when I was a kid. I was always pretty intense, pretty private. I was secretive; we'd all go out into the forest and make camps - but I wouldn't tell anyone where mine was...I was that kind of person. There were all traps around my camp, so I'd know when people had been there. I was always into camouflage and blending in with nature, because I used to go to Army Cadets, and I'm still into that now. I suppose my creative impulse was there as a child too, but it was like a little seed at the time - and it was something that I kept very personal to myself. I was also very interested in dancing because, for some reason, I was better at it than a lot of people - not that I went out to be. I just did what I enjoyed, and found out that I was good at it. So I got into dancing and got into music, particularly rap music. Rap is so easy to do, that I just started doing it. I had a musical family as well, so that helped. My brother Olly was a guitarist,

drummer, keyboard player, singer and songwriter. My sister was a singer, Dad was a guitarist and my mum was a dancer. It kind of rubbed off on me, but my family would do all of these things openly - whereas I'd do it on my own. I was the least likely one to be famous out of the lot of us, but I was tremendously influenced by it all. I also got influenced by such a wide range of music that I think I was very lucky. My brother's room in the house would be beating out Jimi Hendrix riffs, my sister would be playing dub - and I'd have *Prince* or *Public Enemy* on. You combine all of those styles, and you've got something going on."

JOHN

"To be honest, things weren't too great for me as a kid, but it was no big deal. I can't say I really had an unhappy childhood, or anything...it's just that we didn't really have much of anything. It was tough. My mum left when I was about five or six, so there was just the three of us, my dad, my sister Karen and myself, doing the best we could. From that experience, I learned pretty early on how to fend for myself, how to survive. I suppose you could say that I grew up fast. I had to. You know, I'd come home from school and me and Karen would have to look after ourselves - but you'd get used to it because, basically, you didn't know any different. Where I grew up isn't exactly the easiest place to get by, but everyone around us was in pretty much the same situation, so you had that in common. I've always been a pretty quiet kind of bloke, I still am, but I had loads of mates and we were always out and about getting up to loads of mischief - which you just do as a kid. I wasn't particularly interested in school, but I did have some great times there - probably doing all of the things which I shouldn't have! And I always loved music. I was into music in a big way from an early age; always trying to get money to buy new records and build up my hi-fi system. Looking back on my childhood, it was OK - and it definitely shaped the way I am today. People think I'm hard or something, that I'm difficult to approach or don't want to know…but I'm not, and never have been. I just go about my life in a quiet way, sort of keep myself to myself, but I'm just as friendly as the next person. You know, people were really surprised with my dancing on the last tour - but I'd always danced. I didn't just suddenly learn. It's just that people hadn't seen me do it before. As a kid, maybe I wasn't that confident, or didn't seem to be, but being in *East 17* has certainly brought me out of myself. Put it another way; everything I had inside me as a kid is now out in the open. But, I must admit, I am still on the quiet side."

"I was full of mischief, always getting into trouble. Burning fences, messing around. Lots of trouble. But I suppose I was happy. I certainly wasn't unhappy. I was pretty quiet, pretty much kept myself to myself. I was like that when the band first started too. I didn't have a lot of confidence, but I've matured a lot since then. The thing was, where I grew up, the way I was as a kid wasn't anything unusual. There was loads of us in loads of gangs roaming about and trying to find something to do. I look back on it now and realise that a lot of what we did was wrong - and I definitely wouldn't be too happy if someone burned my fence - but you just don't think about any of that when you're young. I mean, I never thought I'd grow up to be the kind of guy who asked people to take their shoes off when they step into my flat - but I do. I don't want them messing up my carpet; it's brand new! I know I'm lucky to be in the

position I'm in now, because it could so easily have turned out so differently for me. I wasn't into school at all as a kid. I just didn't want to be there and I had no interest at all in learning anything. The only thing I was really good at when I was at school was getting detention. I was always top of the class at that! Mind you, I was also pretty great at not going to school at all in the first place; I played truant a lot. Now, I'm not bragging about any of this, saying it's cool to do it or that it's OK for anyone else to. I'm saying the exact opposite. It's just that, when I was a kid, that's what I was like. I hope people will learn what not to do from my example, not follow it. Anyway, after school - which I left as soon as I could, of course! - I had a whole bunch of jobs,

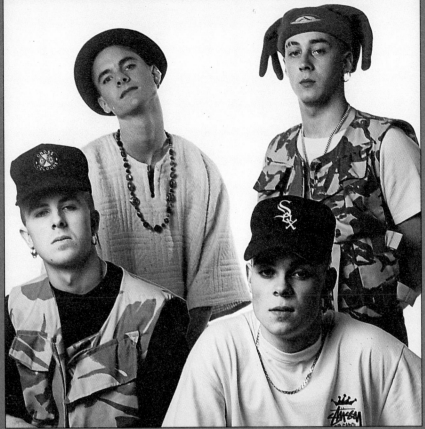

me. Mainly Es... Anyone who knows me will tell you that I'm cocky or loud or cheeky - I'll admit it myself - and I was definitely like that when I was younger. It's not something I grew into. As a kid, and I suppose we're not really talking about that long ago in my case, I was always into music, always singing out loud. I'd sit on a wall at this place in Walthamstow, swinging my legs and singing away. People used to tell me I had a good voice, but I never really thought much about it. I certainly never imagined it would all lead to this, or that it could lead to this. I was just a mouthy little kid who liked singing...I had no major ambitions to be doing this. Well, you don't, do you? I just thought I'd end up doing a regular job when I grew up - which is what I was doing before *East 17*. I was a plumber. If it wasn't for the band, that's what I'd still be doing now; shoving my hands down some muddy ditch and playing around with a pipe. My parents split up when I was young; my mum moved to another borough in London. I didn't really want to move, so I stayed in Walthamstow and lived with my nan. I was about 11-years-old at the time. I suppose people might read this and think 'Wo! That's a heavy decision to make, not moving away with your mum, when you're that young...' But it wasn't like that. It was all I knew, living in Walthamstow. I didn't know any different. It's not like anyone forced me either way or anything. I just decided I'd rather stay where I was. No big deal."

but I just couldn't hold any of them down. I was a printer, builder, paper boy. I worked in a factory and in a sweet shop. I sold bacon down the market, worked on a fruit 'n' veg stall, on a clothes stall. The one thing which really excited me was dancing, and then I was asked to join this group called *East 17*..."

BRIAN

"What was I like as a kid? I was small. Small and very young. No...I wasn't very well behaved. I was bad. I was happy, though - just a smaller version of myself now, really. But I was normal, really, just a normal kid doing what normal kids do. Mucking around and getting into trouble, making noise with my mates and getting moved on by the police. It's not really that much different to the way things are now, except that I get paid for doing it these days! School wasn't a very big deal for me; I didn't really care that much for it. I got in the odd bit of bother there, like everyone else, but I did just about pass some exams. Yeah, I've got some qualifications,

BRIAN LEE HARVEY

1. Doesn't understand the meaning of the words 'quiet' or 'reserved'.

2. Is probably in a livelier mood more of the time than any other member of *East 17*.

3. Sort of struts around the place, with a swagger.

4. Wouldn't dream of being rude to anyone in public who doesn't know him.

5. Once borrowed $15 from the bloke who wrote this annual to buy a baseball cap in New York. And still hasn't paid it back.

6. Is almost impossible to extract a straight, serious answer from.

7. Can't believe he ever had the bad taste to have dreadlocks weaved into his hair.

8. Might not be 7ft tall, but is a wizard at basketball.

9. Didn't believe it when he was told that lifts in America don't stop on the 13th floor, because there never is one.

10. Has the appetite of a horse and eyes bigger than his stomach - but still leaves more than he eats.

11. Now has three tattoos, and counting.

12. Has a habit of taking photographs with other people's cameras.

13. Regularly calls up the *East 17* Hotline to check what's being said about him!

14. Always seems to go out in the cold with not enough clothes on.

15. Thinks he's not bad as a singer, but wants to be much better.

16. Enjoys haggling over the price of everything.

17. Has a permanent smirk on his face, like he's up to no good. Usually, he is...

13

number1

"Obviously, I was really pleased about getting to Number One in the UK singles chart for the first time. But, at the end of the day - and not being big-headed or anything - because we've had number ones in so many other countries...it wasn't quite the buzz I might have expected. Also, in the UK, Mr Blobby gets to Number One. We got to Number One, but so did Mr Blobby - so is it a hard thing to do or have you just got to do a stupid song to get to Number One? But, of course, I was glad - although I knew it would get to Number One, because it's such a good song plus it was Christmas and all of that. We were all still celebrating with champagne for about a week after it went to Number One."

"JOHN"

"TONY" "Does being Number One really matter to us any more? Not really...no, but it was really nice. The first week that 'Stay Another Day' got there I was like 'So, big deal...' and then the next week I was thinking 'Oh, wow! This is pretty serious.' After three weeks, four weeks and five weeks, the thought that I kept getting was, 'Hey, they really do like our song.' But there's so much rubbish that goes to Number One as well, that it's kind of lost its meaning a bit. It doesn't have to be an excellent song any more to get to the top. But when you're top of the charts, you're 'beating' everyone else so, as positions go, it's great. It was pretty cool, I enjoyed it, and I wanted it to be there for Christmas. We've had a Number One album - and now we've had a Number One single. We can't really better that. We can only hope to do it again."

"TERRY" "We were at the Smash Hits Poll Winners' Party when we found out that 'Stay Another Day' had got to Number One. It was a wicked feeling. We didn't listen to the chart rundown to hear the position of the single, though; we were told before it was announced - and it was ruff, man. Bad. The champagne was opened and everyone was really happy. All the record company and the management were there. The guy from the fan club, don't know his name - Mike or someone - he was quite happy, too. We drove down the road one day and there he was, standing in the middle of the road with a bottle of champagne and some plastic cups on a tray. He had a sign around his neck saying

'Congratulations! We Are Number One!' Being at Number One is a good vibe."

"BRIAN" "I was ill at the time, so getting to Number One didn't hit me as well as it should've done. It is nice though. But I didn't feel like Number One. I suppose I was just feeling so crappy that it didn't really sink in. To tell you the truth, it was probably more exciting when we got into the charts for the first time with 'House Of Love' or first heard that song played on the radio. The longer you release hit records, the more you get used to it - and we'd put out seven singles before we got to the top. The thing is, I'm sure we'd all rather have waited that long to get to Number One, as opposed to getting to the top of the charts really early on in our career. I mean, if you get to the top too soon, where do you from there? It's a tough act to follow."

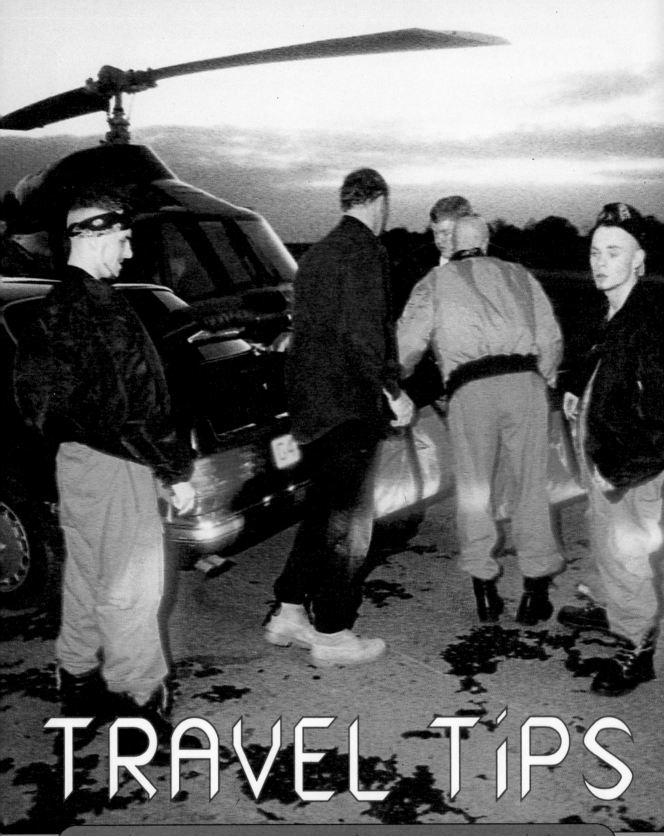

TRAVEL TiPS

As you know, *East 17* are international, jet-setting superstar playboys. In other words, they get around a bit - in the travelling sense, that is. Here's how they avoid leaving town without those all important essentials, being violently ill over each other and falling asleep when they're not supposed to as they scoot around the world...

BRIAN: "I brace myself, from the moment I get on the plane to the moment I get off. I don't like flying, man, and I never have. I don't know what it is, but I don't like it. I don't trust planes, man, and I don't trust humans flying them. Anything can go wrong at any time; it's not a mechanical person flying it, so it's not guaranteed. You know, the geezer could have a heart attack. And planes must be like cars; if engines can mess up on cars, then can mess up on planes, can't they? Anything can happen. So, my travel tip is...don't fly! If you have to, make sure you pack clothes, toiletries and a bit of music."

TONY: "Pack only the bare essentials; not too many clothes, concentrate on the underwear department and toiletries bag. We're lucky because we don't have to worry about tickets and stuff, because John Buckland does all of that for us, but I'm always concerned about my passport, my door keys and my credit card. If you're travelling, particularly flying, wear loose clothing. Tracksuit bottoms are really good. Dress like you're going for a work-out, because it's quite gruelling going on a flight; your body gets really tossed about and it gets dehydrated and stuff. Wear a comfortable pair of shoes, because your feet actually swell and grow in size at high altitude. Also, if you're inclined to travel sickness, take travel pills before your journey."

TERRY: "Sleep. You need to sleep before you're travelling anywhere. You need your pants, your underwear, your clothes. This next bit is very important; you need your sweets for the plane in case your ears pop. I always suck a sweet when I'm flying, because some of those planes, boy, they'll mess your head up! I also take something to read when I'm travelling and a pen and notepad because I write lyrics while I'm travelling. Take a tape Walkman to play your tunes, not a CD Walkman - because they don't let you play CDs on planes. Now there's a really useful travel tip for you; take your tapes and leave the CDs at home."

JOHN: "Always pack your bags and get ready the night before. Don't leave it until the last minute, the morning you're going away, because you'll forget loads of things. Very important is your toilet bag. Make sure you've got everything in there; toothpaste, toothbrush, shaver, shaving foam, deodorant, moisturiser...and a bit of aftershave. Then think about your clothes. Always take clean underwear - take one more pair than you need, just in case. Socks. Plenty of jeans, plenty of tops. And a Walkman. But always make sure you take the right stuff - and don't pack too much. Also, you should always get a good six hours sleep before you travel."

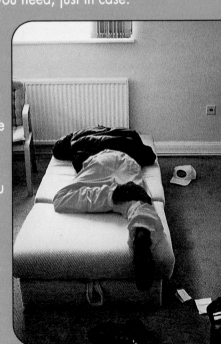

ANTHONY MICHAEL MORTIMER

1. For reasons which can never be revealed, always used to walk into the ladies toilets in Germany because he thought they were the gents'. It was because of a language misunderstanding too complicated to go into.

2. Is the world's worst giggler when he's drunk.

3. Doesn't like to waste money. While the others in the band will spend it, he'll save it.

4. Paid for *East 17's* minder John Buckland to go on holiday with him and his family in Florida over the New Year.

5. Can fall asleep any time, any place, anywhere. For example; on the floor of a moving tour bus, on an exercise bench, leaning against a wall.

6. Has plans to introduce a range of exclusive T-shirts featuring his own slogans on them.

7. Isn't thrilled about trivia, but will own up to a passion for prawn cocktail crisps.

8. Is generous to a fault. He'd give anyone anything - so don't ask him.

9. Goes a very fetching shade of fluorescent pink under a sun-ray lamp.

10. Doesn't believe in security for the sake of it. He's quite happy and prepared to stand in line to make a withdrawal at the local building society. (We've seen him).

11. Doesn't suffer fools gladly. He might not make a big deal about it, but he knows who's on his side.

12. Is a terrible flirt, but only in the best possible taste.

13. Knows the equation to use for converting pounds and ounces into kilograms. Bet you don't...

14. Passed his driving test at the second attempt. He now has two cars.

15. Has a painting of Jesus Christ in his house, with eyes that follow you around the room.

16. Has the briefest little attention span. He'll talk about one thing, and be thinking about something else.

17. Lost an awful lot of money when 'Stay Another Day' went to Number One. He had planned to wager £1000 on the record getting to the top, at odds of 60-1, but never placed the bet!

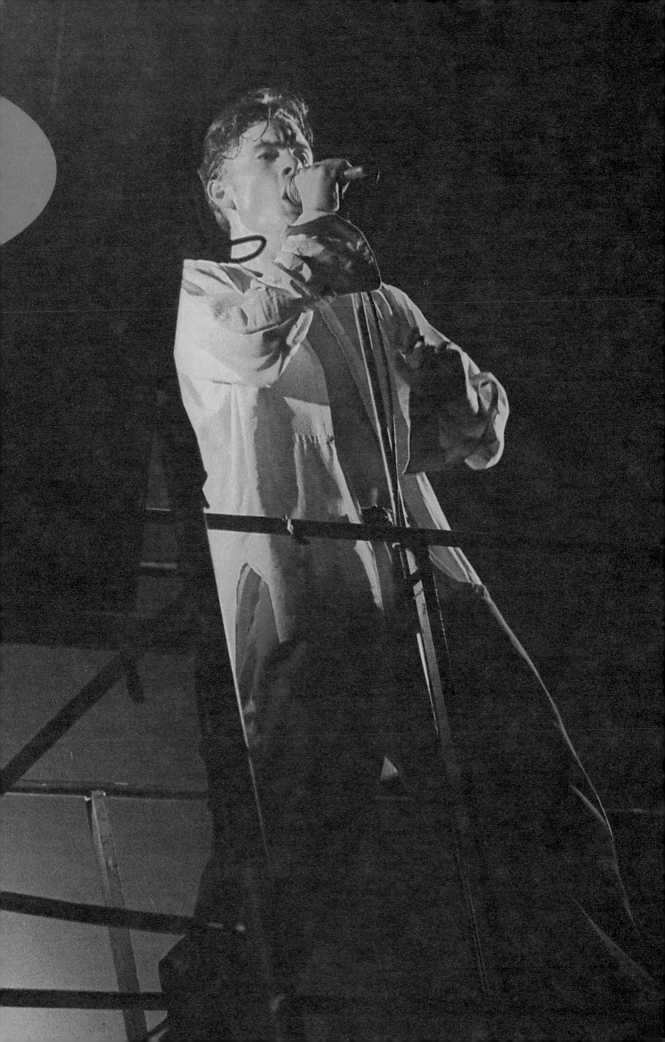

TONY: "Oooh...I don't really want to say very much about that, if you don't mind. It's...private. I think everybody knows I've got a girlfriend and a baby girl and a home which we all live in. I think that's all they really need to know, as well."

HOME, FRIENDS & FAMILY

JOHN: "To tell you the truth, we don't really get the time for our friends and family any more. Me and my girlfriend, when we get the time we just see each other. I'm always so busy working that if I get home at about ... and manage to spend three or four hours with her, then I'm doing well. A lot of the time I'm not even in the country, let alone at home. So when I go away for three or four days, when I get home I want to see my girlfriend before I see anyone else - and then I'm off again. I have to wait until we get two or three days off - and then you can go and visit people. It's hard, man, but I like to keep in touch with my family and friends if I can."

TERRY: "Moving into my flat, and being away from home for the first time, felt kind of weird first of all. The first few days I really missed my mum and all of that. But now it's really good, it means I can have all of my friends around any time I like, without having to ask anyone. I'm still trying to make my home, and it's hard work. You get to realise that all of the things you take for granted - getting your washing done, cleaning up - now have to be done by you. If you want a knife and fork, you better make sure you've got some in the house. I seem to have spent money on nothing but spoons and pots and pans. It's a small price to pay for your freedom though, I suppose."

BRIAN: "Friends and family are very important to me. When you go back home after you've been away for a little while, you get back in touch with who you really are. If you don't go back home, to where you come from, you can lose yourself a bit, I think. Maybe you'll start getting a bit above yourself, but if you go back with your mates they'll put you back on the level again. I've just got myself a flat of my own for the first time, which is nice, but it's still in the area I come from - just up the road from Walthamstow. It's good, you know? I can have all of my mates around and make as much noise as the neighbours will put up with. And if I need to go back and see my nan, she's only a few minutes away in the car."

21

"SPEAK YOUR MIND"

TONY: "Speak your mind! Well, this is a heavy one, isn't it? Whose idea was it for this to be a section in this annual? Oh, it was mine, was it? Fair enough. No problem. In that case I'll speak my mind. Dear me...it's not easy, is it? Better do a stream of consciousness thing; just let the words flow. Right now, and always, what I'm thinking about, what's in my head is...love. Hate. Black. White. Peace. Respect. Mother. Father. Child. God. War. Sex. Songs. Good. Bad. Evil. Racism. Sexism. Ism-ism. Success. Failure. Beauty. Ugliness. Fat. Thin. Bigger. Smaller. Justice. Injustice. Solitude. *East 17*. Craziness. Sex. Aeroplanes. Life. Death. Lyrics. Home. Abroad. Wealth. Poverty. Enough. Insufficient. Starvation. Waste. Friends. Enemies. Work. Work. Work. Relaxation. Sleep. Wake. Eat. Sex. Fans. Heaven. Earth. Hell. Today. Tomorrow. Forever. Sex. Nintendo. And that's about it, really. Not a lot troubling my brow on a day to day basis..."

JOHN: "When I'm at work, I'm thinking about what my girlfriend is doing. I'll give her a ring to find out, and then it makes me feel good and I get on with the day better because I know she's alright. I'm always on the mobile phone to her, I have to ring her, man, because it makes me feel better once I hear her voice and she's happy. I think 'She's happy - I'm happy. Now I can get on with my work.' It's nice to know that things are running smooth. If I don't ring her, I get, 'Why didn't you call?' and all of that. So you get off the phone and you're not happy, which puts you in a mood for the rest of the day. Besides, to keep in contact...it's nothing, is it? Just a phone call for 20 seconds of something. Other than that, I've always got things on my mind. To be honest, I don't think about the future too much. If I want something and I don't get it, then that'll cheese me off - so I don't dwell on it. Apart from that, the other things that I want to say and think about are the bigger issues. I think about the kind of world we live in, and the kind of world my children will be left to grow up in, every night when I go to bed. I mean, so many bad things have happened to me lately, man. I lie in bed and think to myself, 'Bloody hell - this couldn't happen to anyone else, could it?' Everything bad happens to me. For example, I had to move out of my old flat because I got burgled, they booted the front door down - and they took everything - and as soon as I moved into my new flat I got hassle there. The people are all posh there, and they're all moaning at me. I had my bed quilt out, hanging over my balcony, and this bloke comes over to me and says, 'I've got a complaint; you can't hang you quilt out like that. You'll have to take it back inside.' And I'm like, 'What? I'm buying this flat and I can't even hang the quilt out if I want to!' The guy told me the quilt made the place look messy. I just laughed about it...but I took it back inside anyway. So I sit and wonder why a lot. I believe in God, and I think to myself, 'If there's a God, then why does he let these things happen?' I mean, a few of my mates have been killed now. They've gone into clubs and been stabbed outside. I used to go out clubbing a lot but that sort of thing has, well, not scared me, but made me think about things. It only takes 30 seconds for someone to stab you...With us, we're like victims anyway; people are jealous of us or think we're big-headed, so they have a go. Those people don't know the first thing about us. I was down a club just recently, Charlie Chan's, underneath the Walthamstow dog stadium, and some guy got stabbed in there - all over two girls fighting. Why do all of these things happen? It's crazy. You know, when my flat was burgled they took £12,000 worth of stereo. It had taken me from when I was 16-years-old to now to get it all together, I'd bought pieces to add to the system over the years - and it was just gone. Now I've just got a little midi thing. I come in, put my CDs on, and I can't help but wonder...why? But you know, to hell with it. Whoever took it, life's going to pay them back, you know?"

TERRY: "I'll tell you what bugs me. Getting up in the morning. It really does. Especially when I haven't had any sleep. I also spend a lot of my time thinking about food, as it goes. I'm always getting pangs in my stomach, like I haven't eaten for a couple of years or something. I think about all different things all of the time; moving house, finding the time to fit everything in, song ideas. It depends what's going on with me at the time. I mean, moving out really does stress you out. When the place ain't done the way you want it, it really gets to you. Another thing that's bugged me lately, really bugged me - I got a right strop on about it - was that I ordered these cabinets from MFI, right? These two side cabinets that go next to the bed and a chest of drawers. Anyway, the geezer delivered them - and there was just loads of boxes of wood! I didn't order boxes of wood! I ordered two side cabinets and a chest of drawers. I didn't realise I'd have to assemble the things myself. Oh, mate! It bugged me badly. I definitely want to speak my mind about this. I was on my own, and it took me ages to put this one drawer together. I was screwing all of these bits and pieces together, trying to follow the instructions. When you read those instructions, it's a total headache. It really does your head in. And one thing is always missing! You get your boxes of wood, and you can bet that one screw or a bolt or something that you really need to finish the job hasn't been put in the kit. I reckon someone does that on purpose; they pack the boxes up but leave out the odd screw just for a laugh. But I wasn't laughing. I was screaming! Seriously. I was trying to put this thing together, trying to follow the instructions, missing a screw - and screaming out loud, all on my own. I was just going to pick up the lot and lob it through a wall, man. Now that I've got that off my chest, I feel pretty good about life. I've got my problems, I have my good days and bad days, same as everybody else."

BRIAN: "I've always got stuff on my mind and, right now, the thing that's really making me wonder is 'How can I make my car stereo system louder?' (Note: Solving this particular problem is likely to prove very taxing to Brian for a very long time. The reason why is simple; it is not possible to make Brian's car stereo system any louder. As it is, there's barely enough room in his car for any passengers due to the space taken up by several huge speakers. The sound booming forth from them is probably equivalent to the amount of noise coming at you in the middle of an *East 17* concert. In short, Brian's car stereo system makes his motor seem like a mobile disco. Brian's car stereo system can be heard all over East London...when Brian's car is being driven along in West London. I know; I've heard it.) Apart from that, obviously, I do think about deeper issues, of course. Like, 'How can I make the bass sound on my car stereo system deeper?' It'd be nice to have it so deep that, all of a sudden, the car would just lift off the road and float. But, seriously, I'm always thinking about something or other; there's a lot to think about in this job. Obviously, if I'm upset by something, then that will play on my mind - especially if there's nothing I can do about it because I'm away travelling. Ideas for songs and lyrics are always running through my head as well. Anyone who spends any time around me will also tell you that I'm forever singing out loud. I've always got a melody or a tune going through my brain, whether it's one of our songs, somebody else's or just a vocal line I've made up on the spot. The thing about this job is that, usually, you're just so busy that it's tempting to just think about nothing when you're not working. Of course, that never turns out to be the case; when you've got a bit of time to yourself at last, the old brain goes into overload. And that bugs me, for sure."

EAT 17

It's not all fast food and room service for *East 17*; the guys are quite capable of cooking up a storm in the kitchen. So here, for the first time anywhere ever in the world, *East 17* share their very own, very tasty personal favourite recipes with you...

MORTIMER'S PROTEIN PACKER

TONY: "You get a large potato. You wash it, cut it down the middle and put it in the microwave for 20 minutes. While it's in there, get a tin of tuna - tuna lite! - put that in a bowl with loads and loads of salad cream. Chuck in some sweet corn, hot or cold, and then mix it all together to make a nice cementy-looking blend. Take the potato out of the microwave, put it in the oven for ten minutes, just to brown, take it out, put some butter down the middle of it and add the mix. Eat it up real quick, because it's truly kickin'."

STEAK A LA HENDY

JOHN: "Get a nice bit of steak, and beat it up a bit with one of those beating hammers. Get some white wine and some gravy. Chop up some green peppers and put them and some white wine in the gravy. Mix it all up. Chop up some mushrooms and add them to the mixture. In the meantime, of course, you have to be cooking the steak; either grill it or fry it. Then you pour all of the sauce over the steak, serve it up with some veg - and you're away. Love-ly!"

TERRY'S RUDE BOY EGGSTACY

TERRY: "Get out your eggs, right? A few of 'em. Crack 'em into a dish with a bit of milk, some salt and pepper and a few herbs and spices. Whisk it all up. Check out your fridge; see what's in it. Hopefully, you'll find some cheese; grate it. Maybe there'll be some ham or tomatoes or onions and stuff. Chop it all up and chuck it in with the eggs. Put the whole lot - whatever you fancy adding to the mix - into a saucepan with some butter in. Stir it all up and cook until it's ready. Taste-eee!"

HARVEY'S SEAFOOD SURPRISE

BRIAN: "I know what's well nice. Grab a loaf of sliced bread, take a couple of slices out and spread it thickly with some seafood sauce, like it was butter. You can buy the sauce at any major supermarket, madam. Then, you know those Dairylea cheese slices? Get some of those and put them on to one of the slices, and whack the other slice of bread on top. And there it is. The surprise bit is that Harvey's Seafood Surprise hasn't actually got any seafood in it. But it does taste blindin'. Why don't you try it at home, reader?"

BONUS RECIPE OF THE DAY: STIR-FRY HARVEY STYLEE

BRIAN: "Get a wok. Now, I like buying stuff like sweet and sour pork - sling some in the wok along with some stir-fry vegetables or rice. I like putting my own bits in, as well, like five spice. Squeeze a bit of lemon in there, as well, to bring out the different textures and mixtures. Sling a bit of tomato puree in there and that, and there it is."

JONATHAN
DARREN
HENDY

1   Is one of those people blissfully unaware of how loud they're singing along to a song when he's listening to his 'private' Walkman.

2   Has probably got the best dress sense in the band. He's fly, alright.

3   Might look all hard and tough, but really he's a big softie. Although he's also hard and tough...

4   Has more tattoos than anyone else in the band. He likes getting them to remind him of certain times and places.

5   Can drink most people under the table. Soft drinks only, of course...

6   Has very small feet, but wears great big boots.

7   Might like to know that a lot of women at his record company fancy him.

8   Shaves his chest as well as his head.

9   Was about the first person to shake his stuff on the dance floor at the Christmas party thrown by *East 17's* management company.

10   Has had a brilliant idea for an *East 17* merchandise product for next Christmas. All will be revealed...

11   Is probably the best pool player in the band.

12   Suffers from occasional lack of confidence, and thinks nobody is interested in him. John who?...

13   Always smells good.

14   Wouldn't say no to a Bacardi and coke, if you're buying.

15   Wishes he could give up smoking.

16   Is reluctantly searching for a new family to look after *East 17's* dog Levy, since he's never at home to do it himself.

17   Is charmingly polite, and would never take advantage of a person's good nature.

the fans

do, and they show that they think like us by buying our records. It's nice to connect with our music, but you've got to be careful; you can change people's lives through music and lyrics, so you've got to be careful where you guide them. We just hope we're doing the right thing by our fans - and if I've changed one person's life with my music, then I'm doing my job."

BRIAN: "When the K-9 Club, our official fan club, first started I can remember the organiser coming along to a photo session we were doing somewhere - and he brought some of our fanmail along. This was nearly three years ago, I suppose, and the lot of us sat there for a while opening it all up and putting things in little piles. Application forms there, enquiries over here and so on. It dawned on me then that the band was starting to go somewhere and, now, well...we get sacks of fanmail every week. So I'd like to say a big thank you to all of the fans that have stuck by us. We're really grateful for your support."

TONY: "The fans are really important to us. Some of them are actually on the same wavelength as us, and they see things and feel things how we do. That's why they relate to our music. So they're sort of like kindred spirits...of an ethereal blend. It's nice to have fans that think along the same lines as we

JOHN: "At the end of the day, the fans are our main concern because they're the ones that are putting us where we are. If it wasn't for them, we wouldn't be here now, you wouldn't be here now asking us questions, there'd be no annual...So it's all down to the fans, you know? We're making good music, and I'm just glad that they're going out and buying it. I'm glad that our fans are seeing sense in the music because I think people should buy records for the music, not just for the faces or the people. Respect to all our fans, know what I mean?"

TERRY: "Hopefully, you all know what we feel about you. There's not much I can say that you don't already know. We'll always find time for the fans, we'll always have a moment to talk to you - so don't be scared to come up and talk to us if you see us. Bring your camera along and we'll have a picture together - but not when I'm trying to eat or rushing off somewhere in a real hurry! Thanks for supporting us, we really appreciate it. That's all I can really say about you lot. Thanks a lot!"

The K-9 Club is the only OFFICIAL international fan club for *East 17*. The guys play a very personal part in its operation, and if you would like further information, send a stamped, self-addressed envelope to: The K-9 Club, P.O. Box 153, Stanmore, Middlesex, HA7 2PY.

The *East 17* Hotline is the only OFFICIAL phoneline service for *East 17*. It is updated each week with all the latest news about the band. Call it now on:
0891 334 123
(Calls are charged at 49p peak rate and 39p at all other times. Please get permission from the person paying the bill before you make a call)

BAD IS GOOD

Depending on where you come from, bad either means naughty or nice. *East 17* will be the first to tell you that they're both, depending on the situation. We asked them to confess their negative and positive sides...and they did.

JOHN: "I bite my nails. I can't help it; I've tried to stop, but sometimes when I get a bit wound up or excited I find my hand in my mouth anyway. I'm pretty quiet. I'm confident, but sometimes I do go through phases of not being that confident at all. I'm not a natural show-off, like some people in this group, so I have force myself to be out-going a lot of the time. I think I'm a good person, and I don't take my friends, family or the things around me for granted. I'm quite reliable and I don't break promises. If I say I'll do something, then I'll do it. I'm punctual; if I say I'll be there, I'm there at the time I said I would be. I'm clean and I'm hygenic. Cleanliness is very important to me. I can throw a bit of a moody every now and then, and I do have a moan every once in a while, but I'm basically alright. I tend to keep things

BRIAN: "I'm the chirpy, cheeky, chatty chappie. I'M LOUD. I always have been; I've always given it a bit of lip. I like people and I'm very friendly, so I just have that kind of open attitude. I'll talk to anyone, me. I've got a lot of confidence, but I hope I'm not big-headed. I have got a serious side, but I suppose I try and make light of everything. I laugh much more than I frown. I'm not very good at being on time or getting up in the morning. I've got a bit of a temper, but I try not to show it. I'd rather be happy. I think my personality is alright, and I hope I'm fun to be around. But I'm not very good at listening to people. I don't take advice very well; I'm a bit stubborn and pig-headed like that. I get a bit grumpy when I'm tired or not feeling well, but I don't mean anything by it. I mean nobody's perfect, are they? We can't all feel great all of the time, and everyone is entitled to their off days - and to their days off! I smoke and I have been known to break wind in public. I've just got a lot of energy, you see, and it sometimes reveals itself in awful ways..."

inside, but if I'm unhappy then it's easy to spot. I smoke and I like a bit of a drink, but it's my decision. What I choose to do might only harm myself; I'm not into harming other people."

TERRY: "I'm definitely the moody one of the band, there's no getting away from it. If I get fed up with something, then I'll probably sulk too. Some people can shrug everything off; I can't. On the other hand, I do like a laugh and I'm always playing tricks on people - so watch out. I giggle a lot. I'm the world's worst person at getting up in the morning, and I do find it hard to be punctual. If you tell me I've got to be somewhere half an hour earlier than I really need to...I'll probably still be late. I'm fairly intense; I'm easy to read because of it. If I'm cheesed off about something, you'll know about it. I think I'm a pretty safe bloke to have as a mate. I stand by my friends and try never to let them down - although I might be late when they want me there! I've got a short span of attention and I get bored very easily. People sometimes think I'm being difficult because of it, but I find it difficult to fake it if I'm not having fun. I smoke, I drink and I party. I can get a bit offensive when the moment is right, but I don't mean to cause any trouble by it. It's just my way of having a little bit of fun."

TONY: "My moon rises in Cancer, which is my negative sign, and my characteristics are...I'm here to learn balance. I'm also very indecisive - maybe. I'm easily influenced; I'm influenced by everyone and everything. I've got a very open mind, and I don't care much about anything. I'm a pretty laid back kind of guy and I don't get phased by things very easily. I'm very reliable - to a fault, sometimes - and I put myself out for people. Trouble is, I don't put myself out for myself; I forget myself and I think about other people first instead, and that messes you up. I'm very trusting, but at the same time I do wonder about people's motives, especially these days. I can seem a bit distant at times, rude even, but that's because I'm a deep thinker. I often go off on my own in my mind, and nobody can reach me - no matter how loud they're talking to me. I smoke. I curse. I've been known to pick my nose. I lose my temper every now and again. I get agitated. I get excited. I get sad. I'll leave it up to you, dear reader, to work out which of these are good or bad..."

SUPERSTITIONS

TONY: "I'm not superstitious at all. But I always worry about things going wrong when we're performing, because they always do. I always fear that the mikes will go down or, if we're doing a roadshow or something and we're playing to a DAT tape, that the tape will cut out. It's all happened to us, mate. We've had the lot go wrong, from Brian and Terry bumping into each other at our very first Radio 1 PA to being left standing there like lemons without any music. Who needs superstitions when you've got all of that going on? You've just got to laugh about it though, and accept that it's all part of the 'fun' of what we do. Technology is a fragile thing and it's as human as we are; it probably even goes wrong more than we do."

JOHN: "On tour, just before we go on stage we all get together, say a couple of prayers - and then we all touch fingers. It's our own little band sign; you just hold the first two fingers of your hand together and touch finger tips with everyone else. We do that all the time, especially when we're saying goodbye. It's like shaking hands, and it's a sign of good luck. We've always done it, ever since we started - and it ain't brought us bad luck, so... As for lucky charms, I don't have any. I just get on with it. And I'm not superstitious at all - cross my heart! Yeah, I'd walk under a ladder, no problem. I'd smash a window too. Why should I be superstitious and worry about bad things? We do a lot of good things as a band; we entertain people and give them our music. So if we do bad things, we balance it all out."

TERRY: "I sometimes mark myself with the sign of the cross. You know, just move my hand north, south, east and west across my chest. But I'm not superstitious. I used to be. I used to be quite superstitious about walking under ladders, as it goes. Now, I just think it's stupid. Why? Well, it's only a ladder, isn't it? At the end of the day, that's all it is. The superstition to do with ladders probably came about in case something falls on you, like paint or something. I can't see anything bad about ladders apart from that."

BRIAN: "Am I superstitious? Tell you the truth...I don't even know myself whether I am. But if there's three manholes in a row, I'll definitely walk around them. I don't know why. I don't even know if that is what superstition is. I'm funny like that; I'll walk down a street, see a ladder and think to myself, 'Nah, I'm not superstitious - I'll walk under that!' and then I'll walk around it...just in case. Best not to take the chance, isn't it? Besides, it's only a bit of fun being superstitious. I think."

TERENCE MARK COLDWELL

1. Is, without doubt, the conniving practical joker of the band.

2. Has a menacing, worrying little cackle like nothing you've ever heard.

3. Has a real sweet tooth.

4. Is very well-mannered and always says 'please' especially when you have something he wants.

5. Has developed a real taste for champagne.

6. Once invited six German girls to sit on the bed of his hotel room while conducting an interview without his shirt on.

7. Never forgets.

8. Is the best at over-sleeping and being late. Quite an expensive habit, since East 17 are now fined a lot of money for such offences.

9. Is extremely proud of his new, two-bedroomed flat.

10. Is a fan himself, and loves going to see his favourite bands.

11. Could teach the average soccer player a trick or two about ball juggling.

12. Loves to party.

13. Is the moody one of the band.

14. Would happily spend all day shopping for clothes.

15. Loaned his mobile phone to a friend a few months ago - and still hasn't been given it back.

16. Is so laid-back he's hardly standing up.

17. Understands the hard work involved in being a pop star, and tries to get on with it with as little fuss or complaint as possible - as do all of the members of East 17.

HEALTH & FITNESS

TONY: "All of us in the band go through phases of working out and training. We're all concerned about being healthy and staying in shape. Obviously, in our job it doesn't do if you look crap in photos because you're all spotty and flabby - which we are! Only joking! No, you've got to at least try and look the part but, regardless of the job we're doing, I know we're all interested in looking as good as we can anyway - for ourselves. It's a corny thing to say, but it's true; if you look good, you feel good. Also, if you feel crap, you look crap. Personally, I've always been a bit on the, shall we say, slim side - OK, I'll admit it, I'm skinny - so I've been trying for years to put some weight on. On the one hand, the lifestyle we lead is perfect for that. We rush around and mainly only have time to eat junk food, which piles on the old calories. But, on the other hand, all the energy we expend while we're rushing around burns all of those same calories off again. So I just end up being as skinny as I always was.

Pushing weights has helped me to define the shape I've got, but they've not really made me any bigger."

JOHN: "I never used to be in good shape but, the thing is, if you want to look good in yourself - then you've got to work at it. If you're not bothered about looking good, then you won't be bothered doing any exercises or anything. As it goes, right now I ain't done any exercises for about four months, I ain't trained, ain't done a press-up, but that's not because I can't be bothered. It's just that there really hasn't been any time. Luckily, I seem to have held my shape through all of the dancing because, in the past, I was training every day. I was doing weights, sit-ups, press-ups and all the rest of it. And the main concern is, if you want to look good, then you have to work at it. It takes time and it takes effort; it doesn't just happen on its own. But if you don't want to go down the gym because you feel embarrassed or you're a bit small, then just start off in your bedroom. Do some press-ups and sit-ups. You know, my physique isn't that bad - and that's how I got it into shape. As for diet, I've got to be honest...I'm the worst. I drink alcohol, not a lot, but I always have a couple of drinks a night, and I smoke about 20 cigarettes a day. I eat McDonalds, Kentucky Fried Chicken, loads of chocolate, loads of crisps...all of the wrong food. I'll tell you, I'm a right mess lately, man. Help! I used to be like this all the time, as well, but then I went on a fitness kick. I hardly ate chocolate at all, and I was eating good, cooked food - not takeaway stuff. At the moment, I just haven't got the time. Besides, there's no way I could say to you that I eat perfectly. Nobody in the band can say that. If you're in the music industry or the film business, you have to eat on the run all the time. Which means fast food, I'm afraid."

TERRY: "I'm like John, actually; I'm slacking a bit on the old fitness kick. But I do go through periods of pumping iron and pushing the old weights in the gym. Every now and then I really get myself together with some training - you have to in this business, if you want to survive. Luckily, though, we're always performing and the dancing side of that means that you're never in really bad shape. Of course, you also have to watch what you eat and, funnily enough, I'm actually eating better now than I was when I was last training. You've got to keep the protein and carbohydrates coming in. You've got to keep eating your potato skins, which I love. They're really tasty and very healthy to eat. So get some in right now!"

BRIAN: "Health and fitness? Wouldn't know about it. I get up late, I eat crap food, lounge about...No, I'll tell you what I do take everyday; you know those little orange vitamin C pills? The small ones, the nice ones - you put 'em in and they taste like proper orange? I usually take about four of them every day, two cod liver oils, two multi-vitamins - and whatever other vitamins are about, like A, B or D. Vitamin C, for me, is important and I try and drink some Evian water every day, a bit of clear water to wash yourself out a bit."

LIFE
OUTSIDE
OF THE
BAND

TONY: "I mostly stay at home. And when I'm at home, I go for drives in the country, I play Nintendo, I do music or clean the house. Or clean myself. It's one of those kind of situations; we don't get much time off as it is, so when we do I just do what most people might call vegging out. I laze about, but I am a Nintendo addict at the moment, I must confess. I'm hooked on Terminator 2 - and I won't let anyone or anything get in the way of me when I'm playing it. I'm terrible; the phone can ring, the baby can cry, the doorbell can go, taxis turn up at the door, fire alarms go off...I'm not interested. I'm on a single-minded quest to master the game, and I do not want to know about anything else! Those games kind of get you like that. I'm not so sure if that's a good thing or not but - and this bit is definitely good as far as I'm concerned - you can lose yourself in a totally different world for a while and forget about everything else that's happening around you. I know I need to do that once in a while, and Nintendo allows me that escape. In all honesty, if I wasn't getting it from a computer game, I'd be looking to achieve it by some other means. Obviously, I can lose myself in my music, too - and I've got a little studio set up in my house as well - but there comes a point where the music can seem like work. For me it will never be work, it's a creative, inspiring and fun thing, but I do need to retreat from it every so often, to re-charge my batteries and my energies."

JOHN: "When we're not working, I've got my own life to get on with - of course I have. Me and my girlfriend, we always go out. As soon as I've got time off, we do the things that we want to do, the things that we used to do when we first got together and I wasn't that busy. We go into the city and go shopping, or we go and have something to eat - or just go out and have a laugh. Other than that, we'll catch up with some of our mates. There's always things to do. Okay, I don't have much time for much of a life outside of *East 17*, but it is all worth it. It's a sacrifice I'm happy to make but, at the end of the day, this is a hard job. I never thought it would be this hard, to tell you the truth. But once you get on stage and see all them people screaming...you know what you're doing it for. Plus, to hear your own record, especially if you really like them, is great. It's just a buzz. Money and all of that, that can come later; we're just having a laugh, although now it's getting to a time where it is becoming really serious. People know that they can't overwork us or run us into the ground. They'll just be killing it for us. If they start doing that and we work too hard, we'll start getting moody and we won't want to do anything because we'll be too tired. Worse than that, you start taking it out on the people you work with."

TERRY: "I just like to chill out with me bird or me mates. We go clubbing every now and then, but not really as often as I used to. It gets on your nerves; everyone bugs you these days. It was a real problem for me first of all, but these days I don't give a beep! I also like to work in my little studio at home. It's a proper studio as well; before I just used to mix, because I only had decks. Yeah, man, I'm getting into producing and all of that stuff now. I suppose I'm doing it because I'm trying to prepare for the day when *East 17* isn't around any more, but it's good to learn as well. I'm in a recording studio often enough as it is, so why not learn about it? I also like to work on my voice, get it improving as much as I can. So, I do spend quite a bit of time at home working on music when I'm not doing music with *East 17*. And if I'm indoors and not doing that, I just like

to sit down and relax. I watch telly, play videos and records - just do all of the things that everyone else does. The travelling and visiting new places obviously wears off after a while and, don't forget, we're not having a holiday when we go abroad, so sitting about doing nothing in particular is fine by me. If I get the chance."

BRIAN: "I don't do anything very different to what the other guys do; chill out with my mates and my girlfriend. When I was living at my nan's, if I had some time off I'd sometimes go outside and chat to the fans standing there. Some of them come from a long way, even from different countries, so the least I could do was go out and say hello, or sign an autograph. Now that I don't live with my nan, people haven't really twigged where I've moved to yet so I don't really get people hanging around. Besides, you can't even get outside my flat now; there an electric security gate and a security bloke in a little office by the side of it. He'll only let you in if you live there or you're a visitor. Outside the band, I'm always busy. I'm always flying about, seeing mates, going out and just enjoying myself. If I've got enough time off, I like to go off on holiday. I like really hot places with beaches where you can just flake out and forget about everything. I don't really have any hobbies to speak of or anything, apart from messing about with music. I'm well into cars, though. In fact, I've already got one, a nice little sporty hatchback, which I like being driven around in. I can't drive it myself; I haven't passed my test yet. Soon as I do, I'll be out there on the road, giving it some."

THE FUTURE

TERRY: "Ah, the future. The future; what's in store?...Dunno! Well, I hope we can just carry on doing what we're doing, man; be up there, be at the top. Personally, what I want for myself is to be a singer, I suppose. I'd like to open up a dance studio as well. Dancing is my thing, and I've got a few moves, so it would be great to have my own studio. I'd like that a lot. Some of the things I used to want in the future I already have now. I've got my own flat, for a start, which I'm really pleased about and proud of. I've got my own little studio in there; a room with all of my recording equipment, stereo stuff and decks. I never thought I'd see the day... I'd also like a car - and to pass my driving test. But the main thing is just to be happy, really. I want to be happy. With my bird. I'd like to have a nice relationship and, possibly, some kids one day."

BRIAN: "For myself, hopefully I'll make a lot of money and just enjoy life, man, while I've got it and while I can. If there's something I want and I've got the money for it, then I'll have it. If I don't then I'll only wish I had, and I've worked hard...so why not? Also, marriage and kids are important to me. Okay, so I'm only young, but the way your mind works, you prepare yourself for all of that, sort of make yourself ready to take it all on. There's a point you come to in your life where you think 'Yeah, I suppose I could manage all of that.' That's when you start realising that you're growing up. For the group, hopefully Number Ones will come off a bit more often and we'll go from strength to strength. We've had a lot of success with our first two albums and with the singles from it - I don't see any reason why we can't build on that and carry it on for some time into the future. If we come up with the right stuff and people still want to hear us, we'll be alright."

JOHN: "I'd like to be happy, busy, have a couple of cars, a nice home, a couple of kids and a strong marriage. That's the short and simple answer to what I'd like to get out of life and, usually, and without wanting to sound spoilt, whatever I want...I get. And that's because I'll work hard, or harder, to get it. But I don't want much in life, you know? I just want to be happy. At the end of the day, I just want to do this for as long as it lasts. I want to keep fit and carry on, because we love doing this, doing our music, and I can't think of another job in the world I'd rather do. As I've said, we do work really hard and one of the major problems I have is that, while we're doing photo shoots and interviews and all the rest of it, you don't really have much time to do what we're in this for; making music. I don't know, maybe as we get bigger and bigger, we'll start to have more time to do the things we want to do."

TONY: "I'd like to be a lot healthier, to keep going. My body is a temple, so I always leave my shoes on the outside. Anyway, I really do want to get a lot healthier and get back into my meditating properly. That's my main goal for the future; apart from doing my music, my main concern is my health. Funnily enough, it's the music which has got in the way of my health. Before any of this happened and before we got so busy, I was always down the gym and stuff. I've now had to order a gym for my house, which I'll get to grips with very soon. I'm also going to start yoga. I just want to get healthy, and see what I become as a person. I want to live a very long, healthy life. For the band, in the future I'd like us to become more musical; work on new time signatures and stuff. I'd like to make a world-shaker of an album, too. That's what I really want to do."